THE WODDIS COLLECTION

The Woddis Collection

Roger Woddis

BARRIE & JENKINS
COMMUNICA - EUROPA

First published in 1978 by Barrie & Jenkins
24 Highbury Crescent, London N5 1RX

ISBN 0 214 20529 0

The poet and his publishers are grateful for the
permission of the *New Statesman* and *Punch* to
reproduce poems which first appeared in those
publications

Cover photograph by Philip Sayer

*Set in Linotype Pilgrim and printed by
Clarke, Doble & Brendon Ltd, Plymouth*

For Naomi and Mark

CONTENTS

FOREWORD

If you have a name like Woddis you are proof against parody; not even he could find an acceptable rhyme. Anyhow, why should the supreme parodist of our time try, when everyone else is at his mercy? Not that he has much mercy, I am glad to say.

They argue that God is
Rather like Woddis,
Enjoying the sight of so many Vile Bodies.

I sometimes feel that I have been reading the *New Statesman* since the dawn of time, and recently (with apologies to their Eminences of Great Turnstile) almost wholly for Roger Woddis. He is the bad deed in an over-good world. He is the anointed ironist of our age, and having him invite me to write a foreword is as though Shaw had invited someone to dash him off a Preface. The man, you see, is just consistently bloody brilliant, which is a matter of envious concern to those of us who aren't.

Though the Woddis style is subtly ingenious, his formula is elegantly simple. The device of building on a wholly recognisable model, some classic chestnut from Roger's Thesaurus of Poetic Platitudes, and investing it with a perverse contemporary meaning, not only settles us in a comfortably familiar rhythm but provides the whole joke with its sardonic point. It would not have occurred to most of us to transpose Browning on to railway hooligans, still less to put Andrew Marvell to work on a Gas Board advertisement. Betjeman was probably a pushover. But to adapt Yeats to the deadly poignant theme of the Birmingham pub-bombs was a feat of creation, since Roger Woddis has succeeded in making better poetry than the original. I think he has a bit of a nerve milking McGonagall, since as a one-time Dundonian McGonagall to me is holy writ, and not to be mocked. In any case even Roger could not make McGonagall dafter than he was.

Roger Woddis is a funny man, and like most funny men he is profoundly sad. His wittiest verse has the background of bitterness that must inform all serious satire. He sees the world as a scene not impossible of redemption, but pretty damn nearly. So let us play the ukulele as the ship goes down.

It is the fate of most of us who work in the public prints to live like mayflies for the day, and disappear tomorrow in the Files. It is not for nothing that the Greek word for 'journal' is *ephemeris*. Not so with Roger Woddis. He had to be encapsulated in covers, and here, I am so glad to say, he is: the Golden Treasury of Cruel Poetry, the Grown-Ups' Garden of Verse.

JAMES CAMERON

Not-so-gentle reader, look
And you're bound to realise
That the poems in this book
Vary indentation-wise.

As in nature, so in rhyme:
    Some go out and some go in;
Deviation is no crime.
        Sitting comfy? I'll begin—

QUESTIONS

'Was Gaitskell KGB Victim?'—Headline in the Sun

Can it all now be revealed?
Will the dreadful truth be told?
Why were vital facts concealed?
Did some agent in the field
Take his pay in Moscow gold?

Other scandals, darker yet,
We'll discover if we dig:
Call-girls listed in Debrett?
Is Ted Heath a marionette?
Does Lord Devlin wear a wig?

Why was Enoch Powell seen
Taking tea with Michael Foot?
Is a certain prince a queen?
Was the Duke a go-between?
Let the question now be put.

Chinese running MI5?
Dope-ring boss a household name?
Ramsey seen in Soho dive?
Is Rasputin still alive?
Mrs Whitehouse on the game?

Dr Spock in murder plan?
Rupert Murdoch pushing dope?
Secret life of Princess Anne—
Love-child in the Vatican?
Was it fathered by the Pope?

Headlines must be tall, you see,
Whether they are true or not.
Time has dimmed the old decree:
'Facts are sacred, comment's free.'
Who the hell was C. P. Scott?

HOW THEY BROUGHT THE BAD NEWS

BR boosted its fines for railway offences

I nipped down the platform, and Doris, and he;
I sprinted, Dick sprinted, we sprinted all three;
'Good God!' cried a passenger, mother of two;
'Get back!' said a bloke who was head of the queue.
We elbowed two nuns, a right couple of bags,
And in the compartment we lit up our fags.

We roughed up a Pakki and chucked out his case,
And blimey! the look on the poor bleeder's face.
I'd have written 'Punks Rule' if I knew how to write,
So I ripped up the seating and set it alight.
Dick looked out and pointed: 'Ain't that a great tit?'
But then he was always a bit of a wit.

Then I took off my jacket and let my belt fall,
And Doris, she wasn't half willing and all;
But when I got started some berk sitting near
Said, 'Oh! how disgusting!—you can't do that here.'
And I wouldn't be stuck with this fifty quid fine,
If I could have figured the 'No Smoking' sign.

DEAD FUNNY

The Times *described an American nuclear war alert issued in error as 'high comedy'*

They've a lovely sense of humour
Down in Colorado Springs,
Where the air is thick with rumour
Of unmentionable things,
Where the operators redden
As they twiddle with their dials,
And the threat of Armageddon
Has them rolling in the aisles.

Every throwaway is plotted,
They rehearse each double-take,
And they roared when no one spotted
Their deliberate mistake.
How hilarious the laughter!
How they howled until it hurt
At the deathly silence after
The emergency alert!

Maybe 'Hatefulness' was blimpish
(Signal meaning 'War's begun'),
But the cancel-message 'Impish'
Showed an impish sense of fun.
Oh, their word-play is so witty
And their humour so baroque
That it's really quite a pity
We don't always see the joke.

GETTING ACROSS

Tests carried out by American psychologists showed that women excel men in 'non-verbal sensitivity'

Oh we may be bloody stupid
And inferior to men,
But our female intuition
Is more powerful than the pen,
And the cock that does the crowing
Doesn't always get the hen.

We're adept at body language,
We can read between the lines;
Should he take you out to dinner,
There are little tell-tale signs,
Like his grope beneath the table
When he's going through the wines.

You can always tell a flasher
By the way he parts his hair,
While the hallmark of a satyr
Is his penetrating stare,
Or the angle of his elbows
When he offers you a chair.

Whether due to social causes
Or secretions from our glands,
It is Jack who does the card-trick,
But it's Jill who understands—
Not to listen to his patter
But to watch the bugger's hands.

SONG OF A PLEBUTANTE

Oh Mumsy, it's the starters of the Season
  And here I am with not a thing to wear;
If I'm lucky I may stumble
On a T-shirt in a jumble
  That won't look *too* outrageous in Sloane Square.

I know we really can't afford a party,
  With unions pushing Britain down the drain,
And I'm sorry poor old Daddy
Has to borrow from his caddie
  And cycle to the City in the rain.

I've had a teeny *tête-à-tête* with Tanya;
  She couldn't fit me in at her boutique,
So I've joined the ranks of labour
With an office job at Faber,
  And they're starting me at forty pounds a week.

Oh getting up at eight won't be too ghastly
  (Fiona says that filing can be fun),
But the times they are a-changing
And the marriage you're arranging
  Will have to wait until I'm twenty-one.

Oh Mumsy, please stop crying, there's a darling,
  Oh Daddy, I can't bear it if you shout;
But if Quentin Crisp can do it
There can't be that much to it,
  And nothing's going to stop *me* coming out!

BY ALL ACCOUNTS

Barclay's Bank gave its male staff crash courses in beauty treatment, so that they could present a more attractive image to the public

I know a bank where tellers paint their toes,
And clients wink: 'I think he's one of those',
Where the branch manager may reign supreme
Among the jars of moisturising cream:
There serve the cashiers, bushy-tailed and bright,
Whose lacquered hair is all for your delight;
And there the local grocer paying in
Will wish he had so delicate a skin,
And borrowers trust private enterprise
Less than the promise of mascara'd eyes.
Take heart, you seekers of an overdraft,
From products of the cosmetician's craft;
And even while you talk of shares and scrips,
Admire the fullness of those Cupid lips,
The rich apparel that proclaims the man,
The magic of that artificial tan.
Compare the puckers in your pocket-book
With his unwrinkled, ever-youthful look,
And should, with age, your facial muscles sag,
Draw comfort from the deputy in drag.
Astringent lotion can do more than bread
To clear accounts forever in the red,
And if you suffer blemishes and boils,
Let beauty-care replace your natural oils,
Let makeup mask the system's fall from grace
And hide its spotty and unpleasant face.

LOVE SONG
(APOLOGIES TO SIR JOHN BETJEMAN)

On the Queen's visit to Yugoslavia

Elizabeth R, Elizabeth R,
Leaving me grieving by flying so far,
Whatever induced you to swallow the bait
And fall for the wiles of a Communist state?

Love tugs at my heart-strings, oh! glamorous Queen,
The grace of a hunter, the face on my screen,
How *could* you succumb to a five-pointed star?
I am sad at your visit, Elizabeth R.

Elizabeth R, Elizabeth R,
I watched you arrive and drive off in a car.
You chatted with Tito and patted his knee,
But my light-headed Sovereign had no smiles for me.

And now you're hobnobbing with Yugoslav plebs,
The loss that is London's is hardly Zagreb's,
Your people forgotten, no modesty curbs
Your newly-found passion for Croats and Serbs.

Oh! how could you do it, Elizabeth R?
You know how uncultured those partisans are.
I'd toast you in verse for my usual fee
But a glass of plum-brandy's not my cup of tea.

I saluted your statue and bowed to your bust,
But that was before your betrayal of trust,
And now I am tempted to bellow 'hurrah!'
For the students of Stirling, Elizabeth R!

DRIVE ON

A garage mechanic who runs a crash recovery service for police avoided a driving ban on the grounds that it would cause hardship

The chief defect of Ginger Ted
Was hitting ladies on the head,
A hobby that he much enjoyed,
Although he'd never heard of Freud.
By following his favourite sport,
He ended up one day in court.
The magistrate, with tear-stained face,
Remarked, 'This is a tragic case,
But I shall take a lenient view,
Considering the job you do.

'I doubt the good that virtue does:
It only disemploys the fuzz,
And parsons would grow spectre-thin,
Were they not subsidised by sin.
Our TV screens would be quite blank
If villains never robbed a bank;
And judges too, upon my soul,
Would very soon be on the dole.
Indeed, society would collapse
But for the efforts of you chaps.'

And so it was that Ginger Ted
Was fined a paltry sum instead,
And after being made a Lord
Went on to win the Duke's Award.

QUEEN'S RANSOM

'You cannot imagine the Queen or her husband going out and earning a wage.'—Sir Michael Adeane, the Queen's private secretary

Christmas is coming,
The Sovereign is skint,
Who'll add a million
To the Royal Mint?

She really has an awful job
And does it bravely too:
Just think of all the boring things
She's called upon to do,
Like shaking hands and launching ships
And duties even duller,
So different from the rest of us
Whose lives are full of colour.

The thrill of working at a bench,
The joys of lathe or loom
Are not for her, nor teaching sums
To forty in a room;
And commoners who reap the fruits
Of lucrative careers
Are choking on this latest news
And fighting back their tears.

Considering the gap between
Her workload and her fees,
It's hard for us to turn her down,
And harder for MPs.
And even though we raise her pay
She'll still be in the red,
As any chap may clearly see
By standing on his head.

Christmas is coming,
The Sovereign is broke,
Who isn't laughing
At a tasteless joke?

THE FIRE NEXT DOOR

'There can be no question that Dr Kissinger, the Secretary of State, provided Mr Ford with the robust answer on Chile and the CIA. The Secretary of State professes to believe he acted to save democracy in Chile.'—The Times

In olden days, when Colt was king,
Before the West began to Wayne
And outlaws hung from every tree,
They sent the US Cavalry,
Whose cure for every ill would be
A bullet in the brain.

And after every pipe of peace
Another Redskin bit the dust,
Their children and their wives as well,
Who comprehended as they fell
The truth few others lived to tell
Who thought their cause was just.

Still later, as the need arose,
And using more efficient means,
When simple people said their prayers
For equal rights and equal shares
And claimed the land they tilled as theirs,
They sent in the Marines.

A robust answer must be made
To those who fail to bend the knee:
Ten million dollars wisely spent
To overthrow a government,
However lawful, shows intent
To save democracy.

The methods change but not the aims,
And there is nothing to discuss
That touches on the CIA:
The fate of Chileans today,
If Dr Strangelove has his way,
Tomorrow comes to us.

UNTO CAESAR

'Church may sell shares in S. African goldmines'—Times *headline*

Gold moves in a mysterious way,
  Its wonders to perform,
But men who know the state of play
  Must bow before the storm.

Deep in unfathomable mines,
  Where slaves deploy their skill,
The Church at last has read the signs,
  Or promised that it will.

High-minded men may loose their hold
  On seventy thousand shares;
Meanwhile Consolidated Gold
  Is worthy of our prayers.

Judge not the Church with undue zeal,
  Nor mourn its fall from grace,
If now and then it should reveal
  Its more unpleasant face.

Its purposes are sure and sound,
  And easy to discern:
The seed is sown in fertile ground
  That yields the best return.

What shall it profit any man
  If he shall gain his soul,
And making like an Anglican
  Lose his investment whole?

DOCTOR FELL'S DILEMMA

These lines describe—and mark them well—
The sorry fate of Dr Fell,
A man whose conscience made him loth
To break the Hippocratic oath.
He always put his patients first
By warning those who feared the worst:
'Unless they raise the going rate,
I may be forced to emigrate.'

One evening, as he sucked his briar,
His house on Highgate Hill caught fire,
And, praying for an open line,
He quickly dialled 999.
The girl replied: 'What service, sir,
Do you, in simple terms, prefer?'
The doctor answered, feeling sick:
'The Fire Brigade—and make it quick!'

He heard the operator's voice:
'You realise you have a choice—
The public service, free to all,
With firemen tramping through the hall,
And axes hacking at the stair
And water, water everywhere;
But as your case is not unique,
They may not come till Thursday week.'

Alas, the frantic Doctor Fell
Could only splutter: 'What the hell—!'
Before the girl, in accents bland,
Informed him: 'On the other hand,
We have a private system too,
Which means you needn't join the queue.'
The doctor failed to see the joke,
And watched his house go up in smoke.

BIG DEAL

On the return of Harold Wilson from trade talks in Russia

Welcome to the wizard back from distant Moscow,
Flying home with promises of mutual aid,
With a kiss from Kosygin,
A hug from Brezhnev,
And big fat contracts for our export trade.

Technical and cultural cooperation,
Rapturously toasted in champagne and kvass,
With a cargo of timber,
Textiles, ethylene,
Wide-ranging table-talks and natural gas.

Russians offered credits worth a thousand million,
Lots of lovely goodies in the years to come,
With a cargo of dancers,
Athletes, scientists,
Richter, baggy suits and Georgian rum.

Meetings in the Kremlin with a full agenda,
Zipping through the topics as the snowflakes fall,
With a cargo of raisins,
And nuts to Europe,
Cars and chemicals and jobs for all.

Rusty British freighter with a broken compass,
Leaking from the bulkheads as the captain prays,
With a cargo of gum-drops,
Monocles, moustache-wax,
Nail-files, tennis-balls and Pinter plays.

COALS OF FIRE

It's not a pleasant life, admitted,
Being a sort of human mole,
But then, you know, these chaps are fitted
By dint of birth to dig the coal,
And none too bright, in fact slow-witted,
Though pretty decent on the whole.

It's not an easy job to master,
Oh yes, there's dirt and danger too;
They may end up with legs in plaster
After the roof has fallen through,
But when they die in some disaster
It's never more than one or two.

Inured to pain through their upbringing,
Rejoicing on the morning shift,
They're kind to dogs and fond of singing,
For which they have a special gift,
And even when the bells are ringing
You hear them laughing in the lift.

The miner earns our admiration,
But after all the words are said
We find a cause for consternation
When he defends his daily bread,
And, turning praise to execration,
Heap coals of fire upon his head.

GODSPEED

'If you must go fast, sing a hymn.'—The Rev. Roy Wilson, of All Saints, Ripley, Derbyshire

O God Almighty, damn and blast!
That Mini scraped my chrome;
Was that a warden that we passed
Or just a garden gnome?

I'm doing ninety on the clock,
The Highway Code's a bore;
My hand is steady as a rock,
My foot is through the floor.

Preserve me till I hit the sack,
My soul is free from sin;
I prayed when I was knocking back
That final double-gin.

O God, this drive may be my last
Along the road to Frome;
But, darling, I am going fast
And dying to get home.

NIL DESPERANDUM

Be not weary, fellow sinners,
   Light a candle in the dark:
Life is more than meagre dinners,
   Thank the Lord for Anne and Mark!

If you're haunted by the headlines,
   Daunted by the working-man,
Troubled by the talk of breadlines,
   Bend your thoughts to Mark and Anne!

Shares may fall and prices rocket,
   Wages frozen by Phase Two;
Count the blessings in your pocket—
   Anne and Mark are smilin' thru!

Face the problems you can't bear to,
   Drugs and crime and VAT,
All the shocks that flesh is heir to—
   Royal love provides the key!

'CONCORDE OPTION CANCELLATION',
   'LIVING STANDARDS TAKE A DIVE';
Anne and Mark are our salvation,
   Think of them and come alive!

Britain falls beneath the hammer,
   Outlook bleak and tempers thin:
Anne and Mark will still the clamour,
   Wedding bells will drown the din!

Are we short of Gilead ointment?
   Is there no physician there?
Cupid now by Royal Appointment
   Lays a balm to our despair!

THE HERO
(AFTER W. B. YEATS)

On the Birmingham pub-bombings of November 21, 1974

I went out to the city streets,
Because a fire was in my head,
And saw the people passing by,
And wished the youngest of them dead,
And twisted by a bitter past,
And poisoned by a cold despair,
I found at last a resting-place
And left my hatred ticking there.

When I was fleeing from the night
And sweating in my room again,
I heard the old futilities
Exploding like a cry of pain;
But horror, should it touch the heart,
Would freeze my hand upon the fuse,
And I must shed no tears for those
Who merely have a life to lose.

Though I am sick with murdering,
Though killing is my native land,
I will find out where death has gone,
And kiss his lips and take his hand;
And hide among the withered grass,
And pluck, till love and life are done,
The shrivelled apples of the moon,
The cankered apples of the sun.

MONTY'S FAREWELL
(AFTER KIPLING)

On the death of Field-Marshal Lord Montgomery

I served the Army fifty years,
  I strove for Hitler's fall;
I had no other goal than this,
  Nor any life at all.
I hunted down my country's foes
  And met them face to face,
Until the final signal came
  That called me back to base.

There where men say my name was made,
  There where my work was done;
There where the dearest dead are laid
  Beneath the desert sun;
There where the Rats at my command
  Declared a solemn vow,
Will always be my only home:
Ah, how can I go now?

Cold showers and faith and village greens
  Provide the perfect mix:
El Alamein was just a match,
  With Rommel knocked for six.
The team I led are gathered yet
  Around me in my jeep,
And I shall wear my beret still,
  Wherever I may sleep.

My caravan is empty now,
  My baton put away;
I served the Army fifty years,
  And wish that I could stay.
There was my heart, my soul, my mind,
  And war a damn good show.
I cannot leave it all behind—
  Command me not to go!

FINAL CURTAIN

'Just say this is a comedy of errors.'—President Nixon on a White House tape

Oh, say can you hear
On the Watergate tapes
That I gave to the Judge
How I lied like a trooper?
When the chips are all down
I guess no one escapes;
I've a date at high noon,
And I'm no Gary Cooper.
If they're going to impeach
There's no gun I can reach,
So I may as well quit
With a heart-rending speech.
Oh, say does that flag
That I've dirtied still wave?
If I play my cards right,
There's some loot I can save.

Oh, this is the crunch,
I may have to resign,
But those bums are dead wrong
If they think I'm defeated.
When they pension me off
At the end of the line
And my taxes are paid,
They can (passage deleted).
I'm not out of the woods,
But I've still got the goods,
Though I may go to jail
With the rest of the hoods.
George Washington's dead,
Like the pledge that I gave,
But if he were alive
He would turn in his grave.

VORSTER'S VIEW
(AFTER COLERIDGE)

On the opening of the South African Broadcasting Corporation's first television service, Dr Albert Hertzog, of the Herstigte Nasionale Party, expressed misgivings that television would cause 'disastrous spiritual and moral decay'

In Capetown did John Vorster Khan
A state-run polychrome decree,
Where Alf, who leads the Garnett clan
Through ratings measureless to man,
Would flourish on TV.
A million viewers will surround
Their sets that cost six hundred pound
And watch the wooden programmes come and go,
And having paid their swingeing licence fee,
Be free to goggle at the passing show,
A system simple as SABC.

But warning voices fill the air,
The blessed thing could be a curse;
Discussions or a doubtful play
Might lead to spiritual decay,
Or even something worse.
The pros and cons must be weighed up
And all the items costed:
A window on the world? Perhaps,
But all those fine Herstigte chaps
Would rather have it frosted.
A handshake or forbidden kiss,
A bishop's disbelieving stare
Would make them cry, 'Beware! Beware!
That box could deepen White despair!'

If ignorance of truth be bliss,
Then let them see the talking head,
For they on garbled news are fed,
And drink the milk of prejudice.

MOTORMAN MUSIC
(AFTER LOUIS MACNEICE)

'The risk that has to be run is that ordinary peace-loving Catholics will against all logic turn to the IRA as protectors.'—The Times

It's no-go the middle ground, it's no-go the moderates,
All they want is a barricade and a poisoned box of
chocolates,
Their faces are painted bottle-green, their eyes are
unforgiving,
Their heads are wrapped in woollen masks and their hearts
in Irish linen.

Willie Whitelaw sent us in to end the reign of terror,
Warned civilians off the streets because of rainy weather,
Explained the use of massive force was hardly an intrusion,
Denied that he was aiming at a military solution.
It's no-go the bogey-man, it's no-go the comments,
All we want is an armoured sweep and a bit of peace in the
Province.

Paddy Riley took his gun, hid it in the cellar,
Read a book on how to be an urban-based guerrilla.
His comrades loaded up three cars and drove them into
Claudy,
Left them in the village as revenge for Bloody Sunday.
It's no-go the IRA, it's no-go the Vanguard,
All we want is a Saracen to raise their living standards.

It's no-go the Protestants, it's no-go the Catholics,
It's no-go St George's Cross, it's no-go the Celtic.
It's no-go the government's plans, it's no-go free elections,
Sit on your arse in Parliament and prattle of protection.

It's no-go, my sweet colleen, it's no-go, my darling;
Don't bank on saving Danny's life, it isn't worth a farthing.
The sand is running out, my love, the sand won't run for
ever,
And if you break the bloody glass you'll only make it
redder.

SONNET ON THE NATIONAL
(THE ONLIE THEATRE OF MR P.H.)

After a plumbers' strike at the National Theatre

Shall I suspend thee on a plumber's pay?
Thou and thy brothers are too obdurate:
Thy strike doth put the mockers on the play,
And Natke covers more than plumbers, mate.
Sometimes I think I should have read the signs,
And wonder why I took the job at all;
Now like an actor who forgets his lines,
They call me Peter Out, not Peter Hall.
But thou, infernal plumber, art not sway'd
By fifty thousand smackers down the drain;
Nor giv'st a monkey's that Arts Council aid,
Once ta'en away, will not come back again.
  So long as South Bank stands, or GLC,
  So long stay I—but there's no guarantee.

PRECAUTIONARY TALE

What angered Arthur Stanley Twist,
The former ardent motorist
And resident of Muswell Hill,
Was hearing of the seat belt Bill.
'Clunk-click may be all right,' said he,
'For Jimmy Savile OBE,
But don't, for heaven's sake, suppose
You'll get *me* wearing one of those.'

His freedom was at stake, he felt,
If he was forced to wear a belt;
Thus, burning with crusading zeal,
He got behind the driving wheel,
And though he very rarely swore,
He said: 'Damn 1984!
Big Brother's here! I know my rights!'
As he approached the traffic lights.

The amber gleamed ten yards ahead,
When Arthur suddenly saw red;
With slavery so close at hand,
Somebody had to make a stand.
He wasn't going to sit and wait,
But started to accelerate,
And being somewhat overwrought,
Collided with a juggernaut.

Policemen, doctors, nurses too
Did what they could to pull him through,
And skilled at saving life and limb,
They bandaged what was left of him.
The surgeon sadly shook his head
As, still defiant, Arthur said:
'I had to demonstrate, you see,
My firm belief in liberty.'

MEANING BUSINESS

'Give industry a chance, and we can do the job.'—Sir John Clark, chairman of Plessey engineering firm

Charge your glasses, be upstanding,
Toast the saints whose one concern
Is to see that current prices
Coincide with what you earn.

Industry is such a neat word,
Shrewdly culled from Roget's lists,
No one hopefully will notice
That they mean industrialists.

Patriotic, conscience-stricken,
Choking on the food they eat,
They present a noble image
To the victim in the street.

Pensioners, the weak and spastic,
Gaunt in rat-infested holes,
Robbed from birth of health and reason,
Trouble their immortal souls.

They are pledged to honest trading,
Hardly ever to defraud,
While their boundless love of country
Prompts them to invest abroad.

Leave them to the job they're bred for,
Give these heroes half a chance,
And you'll see the Venus fly-trap
Flourishing among their plants.

THE BUG-EYED LISTENERS

'Is there anybody there?' signalled Voyager,
  Travelling through outer space;
And it focused its television cameras
  On Jupiter, just in case:
And it switched on all its computers,
  And its telescopes infra-red,
And waggled its antennae again a second time:
  'Come in, if you're there,' it said.
But no one responded to Voyager;
  No extra-terrestrial things
Replied as the peering spacecraft
  Took a butcher's at Saturn's rings.
But only a group of green-eyed creatures
  Looked upwards in dumb dismay,
And whispered behind their spatulate feelers,
  'Perhaps it will go away.'
And Voyager released its cargo
  Through the dark galactic sky,
A record of one hand clapping,
  And Bach and a baby's cry.
And they listened to President Carter,
  And the sound of a Rolling Stone,
And they knew the world Voyager came from
  Was less civilised than their own.

STERILE EXERCISE

Sutton Coldfield's housing committee offered mortgages to couples who had medical proof that they were unable to have children

When God created m. and f.,
Like any self-respecting chef
He meant his secret recipe
To last for all eternity.
'Be fruitful' was the slogan then
Devised by Heaven's PR men:
Accordingly He blessed them both
And counselled them to go for growth.

But all that happened yesteryear,
And Eden's far from Warwickshire,
Where those who live in married bliss
And take their cue from Genesis
Must face the music if they try
Indecently to multiply;
For women of child-bearing age
Put all the council in a rage.

Soon husbands, anxious for a roof,
May be compelled to offer proof
That they no longer feel the need
To grow the human race from seed,
And mortgages withheld from those
Whose wives are plainly ventricose,
While all that greets the eye will be
The barren waists of Sutton C.

HOW THEY SOLVED

the Economic Crisis and Ushered in a New Golden Era of Prosperity for All

It was crisis day in the Commons,
The House was hushed and still,
As a member rose with a question:
'Are we doomed to go downhill?'
'I am confident of an upturn,'
The PM made reply,
'If workers' pay is held at bay,
We'll all be home and dry.'

'How true! How true!' cried the workers,
'Let's end this wicked strike.
We don't want a rise in wages,
They can stick it where they like.'
'Thank God! Thank God!' sobbed the bosses,
'There's faith on the factory-floor,
And now we've got this extra lot
We'll give it to the poor!'

They filled their pockets with money
And ran with eager feet,
Pressing their surplus profits
On people in the street.
They moved among the dole-queues
And boarded every bus,
With streaming eyes and heartfelt cries:
'You need it more than us!'

Soon all the people prospered
And the Devil became a saint,
Now that the sober unions
Had exercised restraint.
And the cities were filled with singing
And the sound of laughter spread,
As hand took hand in the golden land
And pigs flew overhead.

CARNALITY OF ANIMALS

Human beings are the most sexually active of all creatures, according to Dr John Sparks in a recent book

Consider the mighty gorilla:
You can pick him out in a crowd
By the size of his massive forearms
And the chest that he thumps so loud;
But in all other key departments,
Alas, he is poorly endowed.

The porcupine and the hedgehog
Have troubles enough and to spare:
The difference between them
Is neither here nor there,
But both for obvious reasons
Perform with the utmost care.

Though lovebirds make a meal of it,
Before they reach the port
They think of other things to do
And usually stop short;
Which proves, if proof were needed,
They've read 'The Hite Report'.

The ram, the lion and the rabbit
Like nothing more than to mate,
Though even they've been known to yawn
When it's offered them on a plate.
Thus beasts are rarely beastly,
But *homo sap.* can't wait.

POST MORTEM

After the ending of the Vietnam War

Too soon yet to mourn the fallen city,
Too soon yet to scan the crowded sky,
Too soon yet for pain or pity,
But not too soon to wonder why.
This is no time for overloaded birds,
This is the time to trundle out the words.

Poignant, tragic, shocking, bloody, bitter—
It doesn't greatly matter which you use:
They all read well, sound even better
Spoken gravely on the news.
When all is said, the question still remains
To disconcert the nation's finest brains.

How could a potent giant be so humbled?
The blinded husband was the last to know.
Incredibly the fortress crumbled,
The eagle yielded to the crow.
They had the wealth, they ate their apple-pie,
They should have won: computers cannot lie.

There is no easy way to strike a balance
Between the think-tank and the simple brutes;
Might and military talents
Versus the black pyjama-suits.
Charley was good and better than his word:
No one, it seemed, remembered George the Third.

DOWN WITH FANATICS!

If I had my way with violent men
I'd simmer them in oil,
I'd fill a pot with bitumen
And bring them to the boil.
I execrate the terrorist
And those who harbour him,
And if I weren't a moralist
I'd tear them limb from limb.

Fanatics are an evil breed
Whom decent men should shun;
I'd like to flog them till they bleed,
Yes, every mother's son,
I'd like to tie them to a board
And let them taste the cat,
While giving praise, oh thank the Lord,
That I am not like that.

For we should love the human kind,
As Jesus taught us to,
And those who don't should be struck blind
And beaten black and blue;
I'd like to roast them in a grill
And listen to them shriek,
Then break them on the wheel until
They turned the other cheek.

AFTERMATH

'It's the greatest victory in the history of the miners' union.'—Lawrence Daly, after the 1972 miners' strike

We'll have to change the rules now,
We'll have to change the rules:
We can't have pay resolved this way,
It makes us look such fools.
We'll have to put the boot in
And back up Mr Carr
Against the slobs in manual jobs—
Who do they think they are?

We'll have to curb the pickets,
We'll have to rig the law;
The men of steel will have to kneel
Before the men of straw.
We'll have to tell the unions
To stop the smash-and-grabs,
We've worked and planned to make this land
A country fit for scabs.

We'll have to cane the teachers
And screw the engineers:
This mad recourse to Wilberforce
Can only end in tears.
We'll have to build new prisons
And lock the workers in;
You'd think somehow they'd know by now
They're not supposed to win.

LINES IN PRAISE OF MR G. FORBES FARMER
(AFTER McGONAGALL)

A Scottish farmer beat the world record by throwing a Wellington boot 166 ft

'Twas in the year 1977, and on an August day,
That Gordon Forbes, full of confidence I dare say,
Came to Turriff, a burgh of fair Aberdeen,
And there did honour to our gracious Queen
By throwing a Wellington boot 166 feet,
Which will be exceedingly hard to beat,
And the previous record he did smash,
And as far as I can tell he received no cash.

All hail to the possessor of that mighty arm,
Who travelled from Buckie where he does farm
And flung the footwear named after the Iron Duke,
Though some declared it to be a fluke;
Yet none dared to remove their coats,
Even though they were filled with porridge oats,
For they were no match for this man, I ween,
Whose feat was most magnificent to be seen.

Oh! it was an occasion for great happiness,
For he beat the record by eleven feet six, no less,
And I'm sure Her Majesty ought to feel proud,
And in his praise she cannot speak too loud,
Because Farmer Forbes has shown without doubt
That throwing a boot is what life is all about,
And even nobler than tossing the caber,
Though more's the pity it was done under Labour.

ACTION STATIONS

'The public ought to fight this industrial action, because it is the public which will suffer if this, like the miners' strike, shows that in pay disputes only ruthlessness pays.'—The Times, *18 April 1972*

Let us speak plainly and even profanely,
Let us be savage and sharp and blunt,
Let us give vent to our righteous anger,
Let us stand firm on the wages front.

Offer no quarter to driver or porter,
Fill every signalman's heart with dread,
Yeomen of England, unsheathe your brollies,
Close the wall up with our English dead!

Be neither tender, nor tamely surrender,
Turn a deaf ear, not the other cheek,
Stiffen the sinews, resist the basic
Twenty exorbitant pounds a week!

Wicked Sir Sidney and men of that kidney,
Militant Aslef and NUR,
Down with their shirking of rest-day working,
Show them what Barber-ous men you are!

Now let us clobber the work-to-rule robber,
Thundering 'Blackmail!' and 'No retreat!'
Summon the legions of all the rcgions,
Bring up the cannons in Cannon Street!

If we should fail, men, to vanquish the railmen,
Others will ape them to gain their ends,
Looking askance at their hard-won wages,
Working all hours that the good Lord sends.

THE BALLAD OF WANDSWORTH GAOL
(AFTER OSCAR WILDE)

Three OZ editors had their hair cut short while in Wandsworth Prison

In Wandsworth gaol by Wandsworth town
  There is a cell of shame,
And to its door three wretched men
  In hippie costume came.
Convicted of a vile offence
  That dared to speak its name.

We never knew an officer
  Who wasn't shocked to see
The kind of writing on the wall
  We call pornography:
Dear Christ! We were much holier
  Than that unholy three.

The meanest thing that we could do
  To add to their despair
Was something that their self-respect
  Would find most hard to bear,
And so, to cut them down to size,
  We cut their flowing hair.

We don't know if this reinforced
  Their sense of right and wrong,
All that we know who staff the gaol
  Is what made Samson strong,
And that it turns us up to see
  A man whose hair is long.

Yet all men love what they condemn,
  None more than Judge Argyle,
Some show it by a guilty look,
  Some with a righteous smile,
By giving men, for Jesus' sake,
  A neat and tidy style.

FUNNY THING, WAR

The Army issued a booklet with cartoon illustrations and a simplified version of the Geneva Convention for the guidance of recruits

Go, bid the soldiers shoot, but by the book:
Pick the right target, and for Christ's sake, *look*.
Don't squeeze your trigger at the gentle sex
Or we'll have someone breathing down our necks.
There's people you can kill and those you can't:
A father, yes, but not a maiden aunt.
Bag a guerrilla, or a Provo, say,
But not a priest, or there'll be hell to pay.
Attacking doctors is against the rules:
We may be mad, but we're not bloody fools.
Raping is wrong, and looting shops far worse.
Always salute when knocking off a nurse.
Oh, yes, and while we're on the subject, men,
Children are out below the age of ten.

Remember not to lose your way at night
Or rage against the dying of the light.
Don't drag a scared civilian from his bed,
Unless, of course, you get the go-ahead.
Geneva sets the seal on all we do:
Oh, war is hell, but so is Scrabble too
If players cheat and break the rules to win.
There must be honour when the troops go in,
And laughter too, like Owen's and Sassoon's,
And each slow dusk a drawing of balloons.

LOOK THE OTHER WAY

When Shri Pranukh Swami, leader of a celibate sect, arrived in Britain he had not seen a woman for forty years

The Swami is much possessed by sex
And sees the distaff side as sin;
Their double features soft and round
Induce a crawling of his skin.

Temple bells instead of balls
Stare from the sockets of his eyes;
He does not share the thoughts of those
Who long for elongated thighs.

His eyes are down, lest golden girls
Should drain and draw him into vice;
The rigour of his code precludes
Sugar and spice and all things nice.

The female of the human kind
Must never come within his view;
Nothing so corrupts the soul
As women in a shopping-queue.

There vibrates in his memory
No mother's mammary embrace;
And curtained from his inward eye
Is more than half the human race.

CLEAN FORGOTTEN

Nelson Rockefeller claimed that those who were involved in CIA murder plots couldn't remember what happened fifteen years previously

It's a valid explanation
  Nelson R. was pleased to give:
Some no longer serve the nation,
  Some, alas, no longer live.
Minds that planned assassination
  Are as porous as a sieve.

Fake blue films and Indonesia
  Leave a staggered world aghast;
Elephants may find it easier
  To recall the distant past.
Those who suffer from amnesia
  Fluff their lines and leave the cast.

Dirty tricks? A dying ember.
  Poisoned handshakes for De Gaulle?
Deeds as dead as last December,
  Doped cigars and Castro's fall,
These are plans they don't remember,
  These are plots they can't recall.

Murder is a poor reporter,
  Ageing killers soon forget;
Rumours from a certain quarter
  Languish in an oubliette.
Memories will be even shorter,
  Snowjobs will be whiter yet.

THE GARDEN GNOMES OF ENGLAND
(WITH APOLOGIES TO THE MASTER)

The introduction of VAT brought down the price of garden gnomes

The garden gnomes of England,
How beautiful they stand!
They grace our lawns and flower-beds
And make our hearts expand,
And after April One they'll be—
Thank heaven, Heath and VAT!—
Much cheaper than today
And make our borders gay.
They may be made of plaster,
The sprites who guard our homes,
But we'll survive disaster
Protected by our gnomes,
And though the sand is running out
And there's not much cash in hand,
We'll stand by the garden gnomes of England!

The flames of Northern Ireland
Are far from 'Mon Repos',
Though we can see our pixies
Reflected in the glow.
We chuckle every time we pass
Those impish figures on the grass,
They help us to escape
From pay-disputes and rape.
Suburbia may be sleeping,
But with an open eye;
We rest awhile by keeping
Our talcum-powder dry.
As long as Rover's in the lounge
And the geese are on the wing,
We'll cling to the garden gnomes of England!

ON THE ROCKS

Harwell scientists reported that an oil source might be found by drilling into deep rock layers in Cornwall

The Boffin and the Minister
Were cudgelling their brains
To find a source of energy
For houses, cars and trains,
When suddenly the two of them
Began to laugh like drains.

'If we could bore,' the Boffin said,
Eager to jump the gun,
'A hole or two beneath the earth,
'We wouldn't need the sun.'
'Expensive,' said the Minister,
'But wouldn't it be fun?'

'The time has come,' the Boffin said,
'To talk of many things:
Of geotherms and granite plugs—
Of fracture zones and springs—
Of whether rocks are boiling hot—
And why the kettle sings.'

With *Mebyon Kernow** cock-ahoop,
They dug beneath the soil,
Hoping the heat from Cornish rocks
Would lighten human toil—
And this was odd because they'd said
The same of North Sea oil.

*The Cornish self-rule movement.

BRIGHTON LINE

Oh I do like reporting from the seaside,
Oh I do like to watch the TUC,
Oh I do like to mingle
With the throng, throng, throng,
And to hear the lads
Pitching it strong, strong, strong.
Oh just give me that good old social contract,
And I'll be beside myself with glee,
But what I like even more
Is a protest from the floor
Inside the Congress beside the sea.

Oh I do like to listen to the speeches,
Oh I do like a drop of a.o.b.,*
Oh I do like to cop a load
Of Hugh and Jack,
And to hear the groans
Over a reference back.
When it comes to a home of entertainment,
Oh the Dome is a perfect place to be,
But what I like most of all
Is a hubbub in the hall
That rocks the Congress beside the sea.

Oh I do like to see the brothers waving,
Oh a card-vote is just my cup of tea,
Oh I do like a basinful
Of Len and Clive,
And to detect the yawns
When it is half-past five.
Oh I do like to hear the gavel pounding
And the thunder of each impassioned plea,
But my function, I admit,
Is to call a vote a split
When they are daring to disagree.

*Any other business.

FEELING THE PINCH

A Llanelli man charged with pinching a policewoman was acquitted after a court decision that his conduct was unlikely to cause a breach of the peace

It was night in the tinplate town,
Eyed with stars and policeman-blue,
And I was dreaming wicked of a mermaid in my lap
Or an apple-arsed girl from a good home.
In my loins throbbed a prude of lions,
Chapel-haunted in the jungle of flesh.

I saw her checking the silent cars,
Their blind eyes staring like broken ghosts;
Crouched on the nightingaled pavement, she sang her rear
To the blood-bellied moon.
The waters of my heart ruptured my walled will,
My wishes racing through the cat-scented air.

One low, candle-thighed wolf-whistle
And I was on her with my fishtail hands,
Finger and thumb a trembling inch apart,
Eager to goose, breaking the unbroken law,
Hearing her squeak as the crab-claws closed
Through taut cloth and yes-yielding cheek.

What was before me was behind;
Beyond the tattered deed, the tittered courtroom.
Oh as I was young and she was casy,
There was no breach, and I was free
To sing in my dark-vowelled blood
The force that gives the green light to the grope.

HIT MAN

A survey showed that not one local education authority completely banned corporal punishment in its schools. Over half allowed girls, and seventeen allowed infants, to be caned

A teacher nicknamed 'Bugs' McClean,
A licensed wielder of the cane,
Would never punish little boys
Unless they made a farting noise,
And as for tiny tots, he tried
Desisting from infanticide;
What really mattered, very few
Were ever battered black and blue.

And though they feared his strong right arm,
It never did them any harm,
For 'Bugs' saw bruised and broken skin
As part of normal discipline.
When beating girls he felt quite ill
And full of self-reproach, but still
It seemed, in some odd way, to feed
An unacknowledged sexual need.

Some parents, coming to complain,
Got this reply from 'Bugs' McClean:
'Why spare the rod and spoil the child?
Look what it did for Oscar Wilde.'
They stood aside to let him pass,
For he was keen to face a class
Of legally assaulted mites
And fill them in on human rights.

A TICKET COLLECTOR'S LOVE-SONG
(APOLOGIES TO SIR JOHN BETJEMAN)

The NUR Transport Review *reported that some women wore revealing dresses to distract collectors and avoid paying their fare*

Miss J. Hunter Dunn, Miss J. Hunter Dunn,
Sidling past with your buttons undone,
What knockers you showed to the world and to me
When you came in from Ware on the 9.33!

The crowd surged around but I only had eyes
For the thrust of your chest and the white of your thighs;
Though nearing retirement, with two years to run,
I admit to my randiness, Joan Hunter Dunn.

My hand full of tickets, my heart full of joy,
How could I have guessed it was only a ploy?
Instead of collecting, I had a good look—
And probably broke every rule in the book.

Around us were tourists from France and Japan,
Within me a voice—'You are only a man',
And there by the barrier hurrying through
Was wonderful, perfumy, bosomy you!

Oh! the sighs that I gave at the size of your bust,
Which made me abuse my position of trust!
And here I am reading Page 3 of *The Sun*
And dreaming, God help me, of Joan Hunter Dunn!

GENTLEMEN ALL

Mr Jack Jones advised shop stewards in a TGWU handbook to be courteous when dealing with management

Speak gently to your kindly boss,
Avoiding sudden rages:
It doesn't do to make him cross
When seeking higher wages.

He may appear to be perverse,
If not downright unstable,
But you will only make him worse
By thumping on the table.

Try emulating Mr Jones,
However it upsets you:
Negotiate in dulcet tones,
And then see where it gets you.

Present your case with care and skill,
Bow low when he refuses,
And show you bear him no ill-will.
Especially if he loses.

He may be suffering from piles,
His wife may be a warlock;
So win him round with teeth 'n' smiles,
While tugging at your forelock.

Show him how well you understand,
Regard him as your neighbour,
And shake him warmly by the hand
When you withdraw your labour.

THE CAINE MUTINY

Michael Caine said he was leaving his 'beloved England' to escape high taxes, trade unions and Socialism

O to flee from England
Now that Labour's there,
For whoever works in England
Wants to grab the lion's share,
And the exile cannot conceal his grief
As he gropes for another handkerchief,
While he's down to seven hundred thou.
In England—now!

And he contemplates with melancholy
The land he loves, and all the lolly!
Look at those hands, those angry scars,
The weary eyes behind the glasses,
And spare a thought for the superstars.
That's Michael Caine; he blames the working classes,
Lest you should think their lot is any duller
Than life in Technicolor!
And though the carpet's deep in dollar-bills,
The refugees still weep in Beverly Hills.
FADEOUT on Britain and the tax-collector:
CLOSEUP of one heroic tax-defector.

LABOURWOCKY

Writing in the Observer, *Nora Beloff said 'class-warriors' were trying to take over the Labour Party*

'Twas beloff, and the frothy mouths
  Did drool and drivel in the obs;
All commy were the leftycoves
  And the hardline marxmobs.

'Beware the Rankanfile, my son!
  The hand that strikes, the wing that flaps,
Beware the Voxpop bird, and shun
  The numerous Clothycaps!'

The Heathkins took the tory road
  Until he reached the market square;
So rested he by the Sellout tree
  And pinned his colours there.

And as in votish mood he stood,
  The Rankanfile, to stop his game,
Came tribbing through the wedgy wood
  And lobbied as it came.

Left, right! Left, right! And to and fro
  He wriggled to avoid the sack;
The Fleetystreet cried, 'Don't retreat!'
  And clapped him on the back.

'And hast thou slain the Rankanfile?
  Come to my arms, my rightish Roy!'
'O footish day! They're here to stay,'
  He said, with little joy.

'Twas beloff, and the frothy mouths

(Repeat 1st stanza)

OPPORTUNITIES KNOCKED

Britain faces a shortage of female secretaries because women find the work boring

Scanning through the posher papers,
Ballpoint by her breakfast knife,
Martha seeks a job to feed her
And give meaning to her life.

'Are you looking for excitement?'
'Like to join a happy team?'
Holidays and luncheon vouchers
Fructify the daily dream.

Top rates and congenial colleagues,
Opportunities galore,
Air-conditioned Eldorado—
Martha finds it all a bore.

Box-files walled her office ghetto,
Copy-typing filled her day;
Now she looks for satisfaction,
Equally with equal pay.

Woman was born liberated,
And is everywhere in chains;
Treated as a body-servant,
Martha wants to use her brains.

KIPLING REVISITED

A quarter of the British Olympic athletics team in 1976 were immigrants or of immigrant parentage

I went into a public-house
To get a pint of beer,
The publican he says to me,
'We don't serve nignogs here.'
A fat man in the corner laughed
Until his face turned red,
I went out in the street again
And to myself I said:
O it's coloured this, and coloured that,
And slogans on the wall,
But it's 'Do your best for Britain',
When we go to Montreal.

I went to get a decent job
That I was fitted for,
The foreman frowned and shook his head
And pointed to the door.
And every time that I apply
To join the human race,
A white man's sure to shake his fist
And wave it in my face.
For it's coloured this, and coloured that,
And 'Send the buggers back!'
But when it's Sonia Lannaman,
They wave the Union Jack.

O it's coloured this, and coloured that,
And 'Chuck 'em out, the swine!'
And that's what I'll remember
When I'm kneeling at the line.

PIPE DREAM
(AFTER WILLIAM McGONAGALL)

'Twas in the year 1975, on the 3rd of November,
A day we shall with pride remember,
For on that day our noble and gracious Queen,
Dressed in becoming hat and coat of green,
Came to Dyce, not far from Aberdeen,
Accompanied by the Duke of Edinburgh, and standing
quite near
Was Prince Andrew, whom we all revere.
Watched by Sir Eric Drake, chairman of BP,
Which millions of joyful viewers also did see,
And beneath a magnificent tent,
On which many thousands of pounds had been spent,
Her Majesty pressed a button to release the oil
Which will free us all from arduous toil
And banish forever our present woes and cares,
And make us all quite soon multi-millionaires.
Oh! 'twas indeed the day of the black gold,
At least by Raymond Baxter and other great men so we
were told.

Then Mr Wilson made a prepared and most inspiring
speech,
Which deeply moved all within reach,
About the oil which would gush forth from the Forties
well,
Without referring to the wealth that would go to Esso and
Shell,
Nor did he mention that the Common Market would like
control,
Which is understandable on the whole.

So let us praise the 240 miles of pipeline from the North
To the Grangemouth refinery on the Forth,
Which caused Her Majesty's heart to burst with glee,
Because she believed the benefits from the North Sea
Would endure for many a long day
And prove to be more than a pipe dream, I dare say.

PROFESSOR IN THE DARK

According to Professor Hans Eysenck, all children are 'born criminals' and need to be 'conditioned and socialised'

Every infant in his cradle,
Every toddler on his rein,
Following the law of Eysenck,
Bears the ancient mark of Cain.
Every citizen in nappies,
If he's not controlled in time,
Has an urge to learn karate,
And through chewing on a Smartie
Soon becomes a Moriarty,
A Napoleon of crime.

Thus the diligent Professor,
Dredging in the deepest mud,
Finds the cause of wrong behaviour:
Something nasty in the blood.
Pat to such a crucial question
Comes the answer that he gives;
Though you think it out of season
And unpardonable treason
To our heritage of reason,
He proclaims: 'Lombroso lives.'

If young Johnny is aggressive,
Show no mercy to the lad;
Do not talk of social factors,
Blame it on his mum and dad.
Villainy is chromosomic,
Criminals are born, not made,
Underdogs must be kept under,
While in Eysenck's present thunder
We recall a former blunder,
When he called a spade a spade.

ENTER PUCK

Greenwich Council organised a Midsummer Night hunt for the ghost of an amorous seventeenth-century squire. Most of the tickets were bought by women

Now the lovelorn ladies queue,
Hoping to be led astray
By Sir William Langhorne who
Got his noble end away.

Now the unrequited heart
Hankers for the ghostly mouth,
Puckered and with lips apart,
Breathing hard in London South.

Now all Greenwich is alight,
Burning with forbidden fire;
Through the darkness of the night
Comes the priapistic squire.

Servicing this friendly town,
Someone spectral stands and waits;
If the swooning girls go down,
Up will go the local rates.

Now the happy housewives boast,
Pumpkin-plump or willow-slim,
How they laid the Charlton ghost,
And what is more, were laid by him.

DEATH OF A QUEEN
(DAME AGATHA CHRISTIE, 1890–1976)

She murdered hundreds but did little harm,
Kept us guessing, helped us to escape,
Worked at her trade, dug privately for pleasure,
Wrote stories with a satisfying shape,
Went down with dons and deckchairs on the beach.
She spun a yarn. She had no urge to preach.

Gently bred, this shy, retiring flower
Preferred the trowel to the stabbing knife,
Devoted daughter of a rich New Yorker
('He never did a hand's turn in his life').
Dispensing poisons, jokey now and then,
She made a fortune and laid down her pen.

Poirot still lives, although she killed him off,
The light still lingers in the little grey cells;
Miss Marple potters round the vicarage,
English as murder and cathedral bells.
Ackroyd and *Styles, Orient Express*—
Names that will stand as long as men confess.

More widely read than Shakespeare, figures show:
A hundred books, three hundred million sold,
The Mousetrap, like the poor, always with us;
She has passed on but still retains her hold.
Though as a writer not especially good,
Her greatest crime: she was understood.

Fiction is fiction, life is something else
And more than a mysterious affair:
Puzzle, suspense, dénouement and curtain.
Today's untidy, and solutions rare.
Whodunnit? The scene is muddied with false clues.
We know the crimes but not whom to accuse.

NAUGHT FOR YOUR ALEX COMFORT

The National Marriage Guidance Council suggested that schools should be set up to help couples with sex problems

He who can, does.
He who cannot, teaches.
Boanerges, short on urges,
Longs for what he preaches.

He who burns, learns.
He who counsels, suffers.
Volunteers with secret fears
Make the biggest bluffers.

Those who've known thirst
Lack the means to slake it.
Every guide who briefs a bride
Wishes he could make it.

Those who feel moved
By a sense of mission
Are surprised to be advised
To vary their position.

MUSINGS

Harold Wilson admitted to a childhood ambition of becoming Poet Laureate

When I was but a little lad
   (How long ago it seems!),
What brave and brilliant hopes I had,
   What unforgotten dreams!
I thought of being Nelson's heir,
   The marvels I'd invent,
The crown of laurels I would wear
   (But always with consent).

What joy to write in triple rhyme
   And set the Thames on fire,
If only I had had the time
   To pluck Apollo's lyre!
I might have seen the world instead
   With Wordsworth's inward eye,
Had I not other paths to tread
   And other fish to fry.

The Muse, alas, was not for me:
   I felt my spirits sag
When I discovered poetry
   Was really not my bag.
And so when I became a man
   I went and bought a ring
And married one whose verses scan,
   Which was the next best thing.

If fate could change the lives of men
   And deal a different card,
Who would now be at Number Ten
   And who the Royal Bard?
If Betjeman heard the Commons bell
   And I were writing verse,
I might not do his job so well,
   But would he do mine worse?

GOOD LORD

As evidence of Myra Hindley's rehabilitation, Lord Longford was said to have cited the fact that she had read Eliot's Murder in the Cathedral

I do not wish anyone to ignore me,
For years I have lived publicly,
Succeeded in attracting notice,
Loving and partly loony.
There have been murders and maniacs,
There has been assault and battery,
There have been minor felonies.
Yet I have gone on visiting,
Loving and partly loony.
Sometimes the porn has appalled me,
Sometimes the notices are good,
One year the raspberries are abundant,
Another year support is lacking.
Yet I have gone on loving,
Loving and partly loony.
I have been in the news,
I have hungered for attention,
Talked in the corner of your room,
Talked at the zooming cameras,
Talked not always rationally,
Loving and partly loony.
But now a great fear is upon me,
A fear which I cannot face,
A fear that you will yawn and walk away.

RUN TO EARTH

John Peel's grave was desecrated by supporters of the anti-blood-sports campaign

D'ye ken John Peel and his famous hunt,
With his headstone smashed by a tool so blunt
That the vicar cried, 'What a stupid stunt!'
When they dug up the grave in the morning.

'Twas the work of a gang who presumably said
'Get stuffed!' to a fox ere they dumped his head,
And the field sports brigade turned a ruby red,
And they tore at their hair in the morning.

D'ye ken what a note told Peel to do?
To blow on his horn till his face turned blue.
'Bring back the birch and the thumbscrews too!'
Was the hunters' demand in the morning.

'Tis a noble sport for the country-bred
Though they'd rather hunt saboteurs instead,
And their baying for blood would awaken the dead,
Or John Peel from his grave in the morning.

SOMNILOQUY

'There will not be lacking people in the Conservative Party to attack any incomes policy as a betrayal of past arguments and even of Conservative principles.'
—The Times

To freeze, or not to freeze, that is the question:
Whether 'tis better on the whole to suffer
The slings and arrows of outrageous Enoch,
Or to stand firm against a sea of wage-claims,
And by opposing end them? To freeze, to squeeze—
No more; and by a freeze to say we end
The headaches and the million unemployed
That we've created, 'tis a transformation
Devoutly to be wish'd. To freeze, to float:
To float, perchance to drown—ay, there's the rub,
For with that policy what strife will come,
When we have wandered off our present course,
Must give us ulcers. There's the consequence
That makes a nonsense of our vaunted plans;
For who will bear the sermons in *The Times*,
The investor's loot, the rich man's property,
The handouts to the boys, the housing ramp,
The speculator's profits, and the rents
That landlords from some luckless tenants take,
When he himself must labour to support
A bare existence? Who would fiddles bear,
To do his nut to keep the wolf away,
And read of graft and gravy-loaded trains,
The undiscover'd rackets on the side,
The phoney tax-returns, hands in the till,
The unmask'd cases of corruption,
And all the others that we know not of?
Thus conscience does make rebels of us all;
And thus the crimson hue of revolution
Is seeping through the fabric of the state,
And enterprise we laughingly call free
Is forced to change the carrot for the stick,
And call it timely action.

IN PRAISE OF PROSTITUTES
(AFTER KIPLING)

Let us now praise high-class whores,
Girls of noble calling;
News of lust and lowered blinds
Helps to keep our tiny minds
Turned away from other kinds
Somewhat less enthralling.

Let us know the facts of each
Sexual peccadillo;
Let us leave no line unread,
Let us see the double bed,
Picturing which famous head
Rested on the pillow.

Let us praise the gallant lord's
Full and frank confession,
Posing as no plaster saint,
Exercising no restraint,
Paying up without complaint
Fifty pounds a session.

Let us learn from famous men
Bent on self-removal;
For by keeping business brisk
They increase the public fisc,
Braving, at whatever risk,
Private disapproval.

Bless and praise the ladies who
Practise no deception.
Other goods, to be precise,
Bear a recommended price;
Why then should commercial vice
Be the sole exception?

SETTLERS GET RELIEF
(ACKNOWLEDGMENTS TO SIR NOËL)

Argentina offered asylum to white Rhodesians in the event of a black takeover

The farms of Argentina,
Or so we understand,
Are there for white Rhodesians
Who may require the land,
And each of them, when things look black,
Will need a well-appointed shack,
Complete with parquet floor
And roses round the door.
The sound of distant thunder
May travel to B.A.,
But carting off their plunder
Will be the only way,
So if Geneva closes down
And if Ivor* gets the sack,
They'll pack for the farms of Argentina.

*Ivor Richard, British chairman of the 1976 Rhodesian Conference.

THE NIXING OF DICK McGREW
(AFTER ROBERT SERVICE)

As the North Vietnamese armies pushed south from the demilitarised zone, President Nixon stepped up the bombing of North Vietnam

A bunch from the North were whooping it up
Down by the old Dee-Em-Zee;
The boys from the South, who were down in the mouth,
Were trying to hold Quang Tri.
Back in the States, with his options closed,
Sat dangerous Dick McGrew,
And pushing his luck was his light-o'-love,
The puppet that's known as Thieu.

When out of the past came the ghosts of those
Who'd stumbled and lost their way,
And none more sick than Dangerous Dick,
Remembering LBJ.
He seemed like a man in a drunken sleep,
Who mutters the whole night through,
While his look of pain made it all too plain
He was dreaming of Dien Bien Phu.

He couldn't send in more combat troops,
For he'd promised them he'd withdraw,
But he couldn't go back on his plan of attack,
So he clutched at a final straw:
'Send in the bombers!' cried Dangerous Dick;
With 30-ton loads they flew.
'It's bomb—or bust! So put your trust
In God and the B-52!'

But ending the war would help him to score
In the contest of '72,
And he hoped in November they wouldn't remember
The gamble of Dick McGrew.

OVER A BARREL
(AFTER 'ARABIA' BY WALTER DE LA MARE)

Far are the lands of Arabia,
  Where the sheiks are riding high
And gold will flow through the desert
  Till the gushing wells run dry;
Yet such are the needs of the moment
  That the lords of Arabian soil
Cry, 'Arms, for the love of Allah!
  Arms, in exchange for oil!'

Sweet is the music of barter
  To the ears of a Western state
That can dangle the prize of weapons
  As an oh-so-tempting bait;
For the sake of dark-eyed OPEC
  And those thirty million tons
We'd gladly sell our immortal souls,
  Let alone a few tanks and guns.

They haunt us, those buried riches
  That lie in that distant land,
And the lure of industrial machinery
  Is the strongest card in our hand,
Though the eyes of the world look coldly
  And cold voices whisper and say:
'They are crazed with the spell of the Saudis,
  Who have stolen their pride away.'

HUMANE KILLER

Colonel Mather, Tory MP, called for a 'humane' form of capital punishment

The House assembles for the crucial day,
The eager members hurry in from tea,
The colonel girds his loins up for the fray,
But turns his back upon the gallows-tree.

Now more humane deterrents could be planned,
Since hanging, though well-merited, appals:
Perhaps garrotting by a Christian hand,
Or hurling from the summit of St Paul's.

Some more benignant method than the rope
Could mollify the penalty of death,
Some other form providing ample scope
For easing felons to their final breath.

Full many a way, besides the guillotine,
Would teach the would-be killers to beware,
Full many a means, that few would find obscene,
From death by gassing to the electric chair.

Perhaps by poison or the firing-squad,
Perhaps a ritual burning at the stake,
The malefactor goes to meet his God,
Bemused by drugs but perfectly awake.

Far from the decencies of ordinary life,
The thugs would see that violence never pays;
Whether by cyanide, syringe or knife,
They'd learn the senseless error of their ways.

The abolitionists, too blind by far,
And all who stand upon the other side,
Will never recognise how kind we are,
And kinder still, judicial homicide.

TO TEACH ACCORDING TO HIS NEED

They are marching out in droves
From their academic groves,
There are banners draping every dreaming spire;
And the pittance that they're earning
In our ancient seats of learning
Sets the hearts of teachers burning
With uncustomary fire.

They've forsaken cap and gown,
They're parading through the town,
There's a cause uniting redbrick and St John's;
And despite a meagre diet,
They are threatening to riot:
From the cloisters of disquiet
Flows the anger of the dons.

They have left their lecture chairs,
They are picketing the squares,
There are stirrings in the pedagogic mind.
Though the precept of the age is
To advance by easy stages,
When it comes to living wages,
They have fallen far behind.

There has been a sudden lurch
From the habits of research
In the colleges of Sussex, Leeds and Kent;
There's a campus epidemic,
For the virtue of polemic
May be purely academic,
And it doesn't pay the rent.

WALL GAME

A cleaning company in Cambridge guaranteed to remove wall slogans in a few hours

Is this to be the end then
Of freedom's finest hour,
The crudest and unkindest cut of all?
Shall latter-day Belshazzars,
Besotted by their power,
No longer see the writing on the wall?

Less graphic than graffiti,
Less permanent than paint,
Are fading words upon the printed page:
The whereabouts of Kilroy,
The absence of restraint,
Are symbols of a more demotic age.

The organs of the people
Are red rags to a bull,
And we should praise our laureates of the loo:
'My ma made me a lesbian.'
'If I sent her the wool,
Do you suppose she'd make one for me too?'

Take up your pail of whitewash—
Urge someone to resign—
And load your brush with extramural wit:
Nor all their strong detergents
Shall cancel half a line,
Nor all their soap wash out a word of it!

THE VISIT

On Mr Nixon's visit to China

See the Great Hall of the People,
The smiling welcome
And the paper flowers:
A limpid lake without a ripple,
Hands clasped in brotherly affection,
The Chairman thinking, 'He is one of ours.'

Red carpet, white man, blue chin.
Prepare a banquet for the visitor,
Let nothing be spared, everything laid on:
Roast beef, fresh water-melon, shark's fin.
Chopsticks are lowered, brimming glasses raised—
A toast to the capitalist roader, Nik-son!

Under the lanterns and the coloured awning
The friendly talks continue
Amid approving nods.
The honorary comrade gives a warning:
'Put not your trust in Moscow.'
(Acclamation from the temple gods).

Parchments fade, the pattern is uncertain;
Re-charge the sable brush,
Time will do the rest.
Whispering behind the bamboozle curtain:
Any stick to beat a running dog with,
Any dupe can be a useful guest.

TO NAME BUT A FEW

Mr Vorster blamed South African students' mass protest on 'a few foreign agitators'

By God! he's bloody right to blame them,
These alien hawkers of an alien creed,
Who infiltrate our seats of learning,
Underhanders, overturning
The holy vessels of our national seed:
They're all on file, and we can name them.

There's Socrates, the Greek fomenter
Who poisoned Athens and the mind of youth;
Sir Thomas More, despatched in season;
A man called Milton, blind to reason,
In hopeless love with liberty and truth,
And each a self-confessed dissenter.

Another rabble-rouser, Schiller,
Sat down and wrote an odious Ode to Joy,
And got his crony Ludwig Van to
Set it to music which the Bantu
Would welcome as a signal to destroy
The Afrikaner in his villa.

Then there's A. Lincoln, kaffir-lover;
Zola the Frenchman, author of 'J'Accuse!':
These are the few who with some others
Believe, like Burns, all men are brothers,
Who point their foreign fingers, set the fuse
And plant the bomb we'll soon discover.

ODE ON PRINCESS ANNE'S BLESSED EVENT
(AFTER McGONAGALL)

'Twas in the year of 1977, on an April day in Spring
That all Britain with a most joyous sound did ring—
Oh! what glorious news did our ears then assail,
Causing our tears to flow without fail,
For 'twas then we heard, whether at home or in the pub,
That Her Royal Highness was in the club,
And next November will have a baby girl, or possibly a boy,
Which fills our hearts with gladness and joy.

Honour also to Captain Mark Phillips, who, I dare say,
In this happy event some part did play,
Which will be celebrated for many a long day,
For they are both delighted, to be sure,
And keen on horses, for which there is no known cure.

At the Brigstock Horse Trials she did not compete,
Which is understandable, but remained on her feet,
While photographers lined up in grand array
And begged her most fervently not to turn away.

To the Royal throne the baby will be fifth in line,
Which all agree is very fine,
And a source of pride to our noble Queen,
Who is still most magnificent to be seen
And will become a grandmother at fifty-one,
Which will surely add to the Jubilee fun
And cause her loyal subjects gaily to smile
And forget their afflictions, at least for a while.

RED FACES

The Times *reported that the speed of the North Vietnamese advance must have 'embarrassed' Hanoi*

Up in the North, where the baddies are,
They blush as they drink their tea,
Wishing the earth would swallow them up,
And a trembling hand puts down a cup
And nervously taps a knee.

'This time, comrades, we've gone too far,
Even further than Ho Chi Minh.
If we'd known the accords in Paris meant
This kind of acute embarrassment,
We'd never have tried to win.

'Who would have dreamt we'd take Da Nang,
Or that other centres would fall?
We merely wanted a town or two,
And as for wanting to topple Thieu,
That wasn't our aim at all.'

The victors press on (surprise, surprise!)
And pray for a small monsoon.
What loss of face! What lack of vision!
They couldn't foresee a crack division
Was going to crack so soon.

Down in the South, where the goodies are
And hang out their bravest flags,
The President, knowing the die is cast,
Calls on his troops to fight to the last,
And hurriedly packs his bags.

MAKING IT

According to Dr William Bryan, head of the American Institute of Hypnosis, there would be fewer wars if politicians made love more often

Ye shall hear of wars and rumours of wars,
Of brother divided from brother,
As long as our leaders, inflamed by a cause,
Use violent means to settle old scores,
And don't get enough of the other.

It's not economics or markets or greed,
Ambition or hatred or classes,
That nourish aggression and water the seed
But men who, because of ungratified need,
Would rather make trouble than passes.

Thus says the expert whose wisdom derives
Direct from the goddess Athene:
The tyrants of history who've poisoned our lives
Are those with inadequate sexual drives—
Excepting, of course, Mussolini.

Count Tolstoy was crazy and Marx burned his boats
Before Doctor Bryan's torpedo.
We know now why men are at each other's throats,
They're simply not getting enough of their oats
And failing to slake their libido.

O hypnotic doctor, who helps us relax
And comforts us dreaming or waking,
You've shown a torn world the true meaning of Pax:
Not brotherly love but the beast with two backs—
The Peace Prize is yours for the taking!

TO A COY BATHER

'Put a bit of romance into your bath by sharing the water.'
—South Eastern Gas Board advertisement

Had we but fuel enough and time,
This coyness, darling, were no crime.
We could have separate baths and steep
Ourselves in water fathoms deep.
We'd each pursue our natural bent
And wallow to our heart's content;
Alone I'd lie and you unseen
Could wish yourself with Steve McQueen.
  But on my tranny I can hear
A warning from a noble peer,
And stretching far ahead I see
Deserts of bleak austerity.
The patriotic thing to do
Is soaking in a tub for two:
The bath's a fine and private place,
But what is wrong with face to face?
  Though some MPs may think it rude
To see your partner in the nude,
Suggestions for avoiding waste
Can hardly be a lapse of taste.
So let us heed the Gas Board's call
And run the risk, however small,
Of bringing pleasure to the verge
Of some unmentionable urge:
Thus, when there is a bath to run,
We'll prove the crisis can be fun.

HANGIN' ON
(DAVE STEEL AND THE CHANCERS)

Top rock stars offered to perform for the Liberal Party during their campaign at a General Election . . .

Hangin' on
Because I need ya,
Hangin' on
Through thick and thin,
Followin' the old procedure,
Pullin' ev'ry trick to win.
Baby, I don't wanna lose ya,
Gonna fall if I let go;
Jo and Cyril may refuse ya—
What do those two clunkheads know?

Hangin' on
While hope still lingers,
Gotta pact
To see us through;
Hangin' on with bleedin' fingers,
Gangin' up on you-know-who.
Endin' our association
Only puts the Tories in,
Hangin' on to serve the nation,
Hangin' on to save my skin.

READ ALL ABOUT IT

On the announcement of one of George Best's retirements from football

There's a breathless hush in the world today—
  Towns to take and a war to win—
A summit talk and a pawn to play,
  An Irish stew as the troops go in.
And it's not for the sake of a Pearce report,
  Or a ballot held for a union's claim,
But impending news of a graver sort—
  'By George! he's giving up the game!'

The flag of the dockers is deepest red,
  Black are the factories belching smoke;
The rich are laughing, the poor half-dead,
  And the government's gone beyond a joke.
A battle is joined with bombs and tanks,
  A peasant dies in a sheet of flame.
But the voice of a newsboy rallies the cranks:
  'Queue up! queue up! He's quit the game!'

This is the sound that fills the ear,
  Nor are the echoes faded yet
Of rapturous crowds who stood to cheer
  When George's balls were in the net.
Bear it all with a boggled mind:
  How can life ever be the same?
Preserve the future of all mankind—
  'Come back! come back! and play the game!'

NOW I AM THREE

On Mr Heath's third anniversary as Prime Minister

Now I am three and in my prime
I'm having such a *lovely* time.
There's things to do and things to say
That really fill a fellow's day:
I wake at eight and on my bed
There's oh! a scrumptious breakfast spread,
Then after that, to hide my class,
I practise speaking in the glass.

I dress myself all on my own
And chat to colleagues on the 'phone,
Then read the press and briefs and such
('Cos chaps like me must keep in touch),
Or talk to people Very Grand
Who simply want to shake my hand;
All in an awf'lly grown-up way—
In fact, there's hardly time to play!

Oh, it's a job I wouldn't swap
For serving in some grotty shop
Or boring holes in sheets of steel;
Somehow those things just don't appeal.
I'd rather steer the ship of state,
With lots of goodies on my plate—
    And Bach—
        and boats—
            and lots, lots more!

And gosh! what fun when I am FOUR!

COOL IT

According to an endocrinologist, we are being over-stimulated by television

Take, O take those shows away
   That inflame my quiet soul:
Money programmes, Robin Day,
   Focus on the Buttonhole!

Spare me from the Deadly Arts,
   Esther contemplating life,
Old repeats in thirteen parts,
   André Previn Meets His Wife!

Free me from the grip of golf,
   Nationwide and Yogi Bear;
Let me not be roused by Rolf,
   Baxter's voice or Timpson's hair!

Switch, O switch that madness off—
   Just a minute—leave it on.
Sleep eludes me, there's Frank Bough
   And I am out of Mogadon!

CONFUSALEM
(AFTER BLAKE)

The EEC's butter mountain was sold cheaply to the Soviet Union

And did that pump we had to prime
Ward off the slump that might have been?
And was the Market's awkward squad
On Europe's butter-mountain seen?

And will the cost to keep in line
Be added to our household bills?
And is the laughter that we hear
Not half as loud as *Krokodil*'s?

Bring me my pound of Kerrygold!
Bring me my Anchor of desire!
Bring me my *beurre*! O stocks, unsold!
Bring me my crumpets by the fire!

I will not say the price is right,
Nor shall I try to understand
Why we depend on Normandy
In England's butter-hungry land.

ROYAL REDUNDANCY

King Constantine of Greece was deposed after a national plebiscite

Wring out your hankies, if you must:
Another monarch bites the dust,
And Constantine, whose present fate
Is hard for some to contemplate,
Now joins those other exiled kings
Who wait like actors in the wings,
Their foreheads damp, their bodies numb,
For cues that somehow never come.

O Leka, living rough in Spain,
Albania needs you back again!
In Paris the deposed Prince Paul
Is waiting for the Serbs to call,
While sad in Sussex by the sea
Prince Tomislav, a refugee,
Designs interiors and prays
The Yugoslavs will mend their ways.

Prince Louis hopes the 'phone will ring
If Naples ever needs a king;
The Hohenzollerns still stand by,
While breeding cows at Ross-on-Wye;
The Hapsburgs in their Swiss retreat,
Stone deaf to history's marching feet
And blind to social change, still yearn
For Otto's Viennese return.

All these have fallen from their thrones,
And now the Glücksburg claimant groans
To be removed by plebiscite,
When Greeks, who have a word for it,
Gave him the sign that they were free:
Two fingers in the shape of V.

IMPURE THOUGHTS

Obscenity on screen and page
Puts Lord Longford in a rage
And every educator on his guard;
But dirt's not easy to define,
One can't know where to draw the line—
If bawdy's out, we'll have to ban the Bard.

Should sex be put beyond the pale
Because it's offered up for sale,
The very rock on which we stand would give:
To make unlawful or restrain
A healthy drive for private gain
Would undermine the rules by which we live.

Nor is it seemly to impute
Base motives to the prostitute
For marketing the goods that men desire,
When those of higher intellect
Display a lack of self-respect
In tendering their services for hire.

Though love needs tenderness and trust,
It's not as lucrative as lust,
And boosting trade can hardly be a vice.
When life is a commodity
It really is no oddity
That porn should have a recommended price.

USS CANNABIS

Drug addiction was reported to be prevalent among the crews of the USS Canopus *and other Polaris submarines in Holy Loch*

We all live in a mellow submarine,
And when we're ordered on a trip
It isn't only the sea that's high—
Yes, sir! this is a happy ship.

We all live in a psychedelic haze,
Which gives some guys a mental block,
But every man knows what to push
When we sail out from Holy Loch.

With sixteen missiles ready to be fired,
It makes us kinda proud to know
That as long as the free world turns above
We'll always be turned on below.

We're all trained to keep a steady course,
Especially when the line is hot,
And if it should ever burst into flames,
We'll keep our cool and smoke our pot.

We're all hooked on the maintenance of peace,
Aggressive war can't be condoned:
Who needs a second Stone Age, man,
With most of us already stoned?

We all live in a freaked-out submarine,
We're not scared of any Commie bum,
As long as we can blow our minds
And half the world to Kingdom Come.

ALIENS

Consider the stranger who comes uninvited,
Consider his alien ways,
His habits repellent, his thinking benighted,
The primitive drive he displays.
He drinks from a bottle, he eats with his fingers,
His food is revolting and strange,
The smell of his presence persistently lingers—
Now surely it's time for a change.

Observe his reversion to ways atavistic,
The savage beneath the veneer;
His numbers are growing, and every statistic
Prepares us for more every year.
His efforts at speech are a social disaster,
He doesn't know how to behave,
He takes it for granted that he is the master
And everyone else is his slave.

Our leaders, alas, have passed laws to protect him
From every malfeasance and tort,
And those who demonstrably fail to respect him
Will probably end up in court.
So we must continue to let him defy us,
Though frequently blowing our lids;
But please understand I've no personal bias—
Why, some of my best friends are kids.

ELECTION FEVER
(AFTER JOHN MASEFIELD)

I must down to the polls again, to the
  infants' school in the High,
And all I ask is a small booth and a
  policeman standing by,
And the bland speech and the cadged vote
  and the soft hand's shaking,
And a blue badge on a white base
  and a Red scare breaking.

I must down to the polls again, for the
  call of my favourite side
Is a bold call and an old call
  that may not be denied;
And all I ask is a dirty fight
  with the insults flying,
And the rude names and the false claims
  and the barefaced lying.

I must down to the polls again, to the
  inter-party strife,
To the right way and the best way for
  conserving our way of life;
And all I ask are the usual perks
  and the right to live in clover,
And Britain run like an armed camp
  when the voting's over.

ETHICS FOR EVERYMAN

Throwing a bomb is bad,
Dropping a bomb is good;
Terror, no need to add,
Depends on who's wearing the hood.

Kangaroo courts are wrong,
Specialist courts are right;
Discipline by the strong
Is fair if your collar is white.

Company output 'soars',
Wages, of course, 'explode';
Profits deserve applause,
Pay-claims, the criminal code.

Daily the Church declares
Betting-shops are a curse;
Gambling with stocks and shares
Enlarges the national purse.

Workers are 'absentees',
Businessmen 'relax',
Different as chalk and cheese;
Social morality
Has a duality—
One for each side of the tracks.

DANGEROUS CRIMINAL

South Korean poet Kim Chi Ha was tried for writing satirical poems against the Seoul Government

Bring in the prisoner, guard him well;
Frail he may be but rarely silent.
Beware his pen; this man is violent.
Hot-eyed from his unheated cell
He stands before you. Note his crime:
Attacking the authorities in rhyme.

Observe his manner, his bruised lip curled,
A terrorist of the most vicious kind,
Armed with an explosive mind,
A self-acknowledged detonator of the world.
More deadly than bullets, his astringent lines
Strike to the bone. His metaphors are mines.

Art is seditious, poems rock the state,
Therefore no mercy for Mr Kim.
Fines are no use, exile too good for him:
Abroad, this enemy could still communicate.
No punishment meted out is too severe
For the outward-looking eye, the inner ear.

Leave him to practise his subversive trade
And no one is safe. He must learn
The public good is not the poet's concern
But spinning green thoughts in a green shade.
Make him as harmless as the humming-bird;
Nothing's as lethal as the written word.

AS PANTS THE HEART
(AFTER WALT WHITMAN)

The U.S. Air Force ordered 27,000 sets of British-made black underwear for its pilots as protection against radio-activity

O Captain! my Captain! my zip has come undone!
God help the guys with gaping flies who fly too near the sun!
From here on in the casing's thin, the isotopes unstable,
And all I've got to guard me is a Marks and Spencer's label!
O life! life! life!
I've barely raised the cup,
But Jesus, once the chips are down,
I'll never get it up!

My Captain does not answer, or flick the intercom;
His underpants were no defence against the atom-bomb.
And I am left to wonder, as the nucleus decays,
Why British cotton Y-fronts didn't stop the gamma-rays.
Just one dark thought
Keeps going through my head—
That lousy limey underwear!
(Still, better black than red).

JUBILEE JUMBLE

*Written for the Queen's Silver Jubilee—a poet-pourri of lines by twenty poets still living or who had died within the twenty-five years of her reign**

I'm tired of Love: I'm still more tired of Rhyme.
I lift void eyes and scan the skies for crows,
The sportsmen praise the pointer and his nose
And the little deadly days, to work this crime.

In the great gardens, after bright spring rain,
There will be time to murder and create
Impossible men: idle, illiterate.
Long, long ago they passed three-score-and-ten:

And helped to work the tides. Look up and see
The force that through the green fuse drives the flower.
Do not expect again a phoenix hour,
Don't throw old blades into the W.C.

All have become so nervous and so cold,
Critical, and with nothing else to do:
In the day and in the night we are watching you,
Pike too immense to stir, so immense and old.

I thought of London spread out in the sun.
What have I done to my body, ignoring it?
I pull it down: its laced straps move to admit
Something that someone else had somehow done.

* See back cover for key to names of poets.

INDEX OF FIRST LINES